CHR ... ES

TWO YEAR OLD

CHRONICLES
OF A
TWO YEAR OLD

Greg Holmes

CHRONICLES OF A TWO YEAR OLD:
REDISCOVERING OUR CHILDLIKE FAITH

By Greg Holmes

All scripture quotations, unless otherwise indicated, are taken from the HOLY BIBLE, NEW INTERNATIONAL VERSION®. NIV®. Copyright © 1973, 1978, 1984 by International Bible Society.

Edited by Stephanie Nickel

Cover design by Nikki Braun

CHRONICLES OF A TWO YEAR OLD:
REDISCOVERING OUR CHILDLIKE FAITH

ISBN # 1-897373-00-7

Printed in the United States of America

For information about the author: www.gregholmes.ca

Published by Word Alive Press

WORD ALIVE PRESS

Thanks to Aliah and Abbey
for giving me such delight,
and to Melissa,
for always believing in me.

CONTENTS

INTRODUCTION

W E WERE CAREFREE, UNBOUND by debt and timelines. We didn't punch a clock or wear a watch. Our burdens and troubles were miniscule in the grand scheme of life. Every moment was a celebration; every word made us laugh. With sticky hands and a dirty face, we would go anywhere, touch anything and get into everything. Those were the days of innocence. We never knew death, and we weren't concerned about the economy. We didn't lose sleep over sickness or famine, and we never heard of the objectionable cruelty in the world around us. Our greatest fear was the dark, and Mom and Dad held us for dear life if we were ever terrified. They would comfort us if we felt any pain. We never knew the sweat and toil required to earn a dollar nor did we care about savings accounts or retirement plans.

After years of living life with such unawareness, we've evolved into a culpable humanity. We've shifted from innocent, inexperienced people to over-indulged, over-spent thrill seekers. We rush through life without appreciation for our significance on a greater scale, failing to recognize our value or worth, and guilty of neglecting our relationship with the ones we love, let alone our Almighty Creator. We've struggled and failed. We've cheated and lied. We've deceived and hurt, despite being the good people that we are. We all have a story; we've all had moments that define and redefine who we are. It's my prayer for you that the Spirit of God will bring peace to troubled situations, mend any brokenness that you may have, or guide you through a difficult decision. As you sift through these pages, be reminded of a simpler time, an era when everything in your life was at peace. Though you're reading my words, you can substitute my memories and recollections with your own and create yet another defining moment in your life. What's in the past is the past, but your future has yet to be written. By determining to read this book, you're not just reading empty words or poetic thoughts; you're setting the stage for the next chapter of your life to be written. Remember the words of Christ, "I tell you the truth, unless you change and become like little children, you will never enter the kingdom of heaven. Therefore, whoever humbles himself like this child is the greatest in the kingdom of heaven" (Matthew 18:3-4).

There's more to being a kid than just being a kid. There's something unique about the way a child thinks and acts. It's the age of innocence, not only because we don't yet know the travail of the world, but because children are not inhibited by preconceived ideologies or expectations nor are they jaded by secular philosophies or transient theologies. God wants to work in your life to break through barriers and apprehensions that adulthood and knowledge have constructed. Let these pages draw you into a season of transformation. Let the words envelope you and reshape your psyche as you rediscover your childlike faith.

Chapter 1

A MIRACLE IS BORN

THE JOURNEY BEGAN ON A MILD DAY. It was the month of May. Flowers were in bloom, trees were budding, and my life had recently turned a new page as I made the transition from pastoring a church to leading a not-for-profit youth outreach centre in a small, but hurting community. My wife, Melissa, and I were excited about this new adventure and began the process of searching for a new house. We weren't successful at finding a house we really liked, so we decided to purchase a home that we could fix up. I took two weeks of holidays and began the grueling process of tearing out walls, toilets and kitchen cabinets, transforming that house into something we would be pleased with and could enjoy.

During that two week renovation project, Melissa had a scheduled appointment with our family physician. On most occasions a visit to the doctor isn't a joyful experience. In fact there is only one time in a person's life that a hospital or doctor visit is welcomed. It's during the birth of a child, especially a first child. We waited eagerly to speak with the doctor, anxious for the results to confirm what we already believed to be true. Just when my patience

1

began to wear thin, we were called to his office where he confirmed our hopes. I walked out of his office triumphantly, head held high. Two months into the pregnancy, the embryo the size of a lima bean, and already I was a proud father. Without saying a word, or making a public announcement, I'm sure the other patrons in that waiting room must have known the news I had received just by the enormous smile on my face. That day began a series of events that would test me and try me and inevitably strengthen my faith in God.

Aware of the fact that, by the end of the year, I'd be a new daddy, my excitement intensified for what was in store. I still remember the visit to our parents. Their excitement joined with ours at the prospect of this new addition to the family. As I awaited this bundle of joy, as it's affectionately known, many things happened men are not wired for. Showers and parties were planned, invitations were made and sent, and this forthcoming baby became the over-indulged excuse for several shopping excursions. Our once vacant bedroom began to take on shape and meaning. The bare walls were repainted, and I dutifully hung heartwarming pictures. A crib was purchased, and diapers began filling the empty drawers of the "easy-to-assemble" dresser that took me over four hours to assemble. I found myself vigilantly reading the classified ads in search of other baby furniture. Even before she was born, and still a figment of our imagination, our house was radically transformed into Baby Central with everything from diapers to cribs and pacifiers to highchairs.

In August of that year, my wife and I took two weeks holidays, packed up our car, and drove from Ontario to Newfoundland to visit some of our relatives on the coast. During our vacation, Melissa began experiencing some discomfort outside of the normally expected discomfort associated with pregnancy. Wanting to be safe, and not knowing what to expect, we made a visit to a doctor in Newfoundland who found nothing abnormal but insisted that we visit our family doctor upon returning home, which we did.

It's my experience that everything that happens seems to catch us unaware. Sometimes the unexpected violently seizes us, like at the sudden death of a loved one. Yet, at other times, the unexpected progressively exposes itself. What began as a routine check-up or visit to a doctor becomes cause for concern. No matter how methodical we are, or how detail-driven, nothing can prepare us for what each day holds. No one plans to get sick or to contract a virus. Presumably, no one prearranges their own death. Any sensible person would not knowingly inflict car trouble on themselves while driving to work when they are already running behind schedule. While nobody plans for it, inevitably things happen that catch us off guard.

One morning in the fall of 2002, I had such an experience. I sat in my office going through my daily routine with precise accuracy. My days were structured and very habitual. But the usual was interrupted as the telephone on my uncluttered desk began to ring. A ringing telephone in an office is not unusual. What was unusual was that the call display revealed that it was my wife calling from work. Reluctantly I answered, fearing something was wrong but hoping for a gentle reminder to pick something up at the grocery store on my way home. I listened in disbelief to her voice. "Dr. Mayo called, and something's wrong with the baby." The unrelenting tests and multiple ultrasounds were the telltale signs, progressively alerting us to something, but we didn't know what, so we ignored them completely until the doctor's call. As the emotion of the moment caught up to her, she was unable to articulate what was wrong, so I decided to call our doctor to allow him to fill in the blanks.

3

Somewhere between placing the receiver back on the base and picking up to dial the doctor's number, my excitement diminished, my enthusiasm waned, my heart leapt and the journey began.

In a moment life can change. Excitement can turn to cautiousness, joy to concern, expectancy to uncertainty. All of the excitement and anticipation that once gripped my heart turned to concern and insecurity. I felt helpless and powerless, obsessed with wanting to do something for the child I hadn't even had the chance to hold or to touch or to see. Our doctor informed us that he suspected a virus had infected the fetus and that without a blood transfusion, this unborn baby could die or, at best, be born with severe brain damage. We were immediately sent to a specialist an hour and a half from our home with the instruction that, if he confirmed the prognosis, we would have to go directly to Toronto Sick Kid's Hospital where the baby would receive a blood transfusion in the womb. As we packed for our trip into the unknown, we called friends and family to pray. Churches all around our area began to intercede on behalf of this unborn life.

As we made the heart wrenching drive to see the neonatal specialist, something unexplainable happened. Inside our little car, the same car that, days earlier, had been filled with joy and pleasure as we packed it full of baby essentials during one of our shopping excursions, an overwhelming peace filled us at the same moment. We weren't afraid; we simply trusted and believed. As the scenery of that fall day breezed past our car, we began to pray, eyes open, hearts expectant, "God, heal this baby!" It was a simple prayer to a God for whom it was a simple task.

At the hospital, the specialist examined the results of tests, read and reread ultrasounds, and looked over the charts that we delivered from our family physician. After a short time he determined to meet with us. Rather than bringing definitive answers followed by a logical course of action, this doctor was perplexed. Without a greeting or introduction, he walked into the office where we awaited his direction. He leaned back on the examining table and spoke pragmatically saying, "These things don't fix themselves without our intervention, but our tests don't reveal anything wrong!" Instantly my wife and I knew that there had been intervention: God intervened and healed that child!

Over the duration of the pregnancy, the specialist continued to see us on a weekly basis. Each visit was earmarked with the same perplexed look, followed by the same statement, "I don't understand it!" "The wisdom of this world is foolishness in God's sight ..." (1 Corinthians 3:19). It doesn't matter what science and medical technology tell us to be fact. God is above all things, and the wisest of all doctors and medicine are foolishness to God's abounding power.

On December 8, 2002, although she was six weeks early, weighing only four pounds and six ounces a miracle was born in the life of my daughter, Aliah Rachel Holmes. What doctors said was impossible, God proved to be possible. As I watch her grow, develop and learn, I find myself growing, developing and learning. Every day is a gift from God, and I recognize that what God has entrusted into my care is a fragile life that I must diligently love and protect, care for and preserve. I trust that as you read the thoughts that are derived from my observations of her, you too will be blessed by God's blessing to me.

Chapter 2

SHE THINKS MY HEAD IS HUGE

A MATTER OF PERSPECTIVE

I T WAS A COLD DECEMBER DAY IN 2002 when Aliah was
born. It was the eighth day of the month to be precise.
As I waited in the hospital for her, I frequently checked my
voicemail. It's not that I'm so important that I receive
numerous telephone calls; it's that I was expecting one
important call. Three months previous to the birth of Aliah,
I had applied to the Chatham-Kent Police Service to be a
chaplain. I was awaiting the call that would bring either
delight in my acceptance or disappointment in my
rejection. On the tenth day of that month, I received a
unanimous yes vote from the Police Commission and was
invited to the station to get sized up for my uniform. In my
opinion the month couldn't get any better: My first child
was born and I successfully landed a prestigious position
(though it was volunteer) with a badge and a uniform.

Until my last year of high school, my dream was to be
a police officer. As a young boy, every Halloween I would
dress up as a cop. When I would play, I'd play cops and
robbers, and I'd be the cop. My grandfather, who is now

GREG HOLMES

deceased, once served as the Chief of Police in my
hometown, and my uncle now serves as a detachment
commander for the provincial police force in Ontario.
Policing is in my blood, but, recognizing the call of God on
my life to ministry, I had to relinquish that passion. Serving
as a chaplain was God's consolation to me I'm sure.

My first tour of police headquarters ended in the
basement (no, not in a cell) in the supply room with the
quartermaster. As he sized me up from head to toe, he
kindly pointed out that my head size was, in his word,
"abnormal"—large, you could say. His exact words were,
"Not too many people have heads this big." I wasn't
surprised. In fact, it's a characteristic (not a flaw) that my
family physician has also noticed and kindly pointed out,
and so I've come to accept it as "normal".

I never suspected that my position as a chaplain and
the life of my daughter starting at the same time was very
significant until two years later when I was lying on my
bed with Aliah and my wife. I make it a habit not to pester
anyone (snicker), but in a home where I'm outnumbered
three to one, girls to guys, I tend to get picked on. Case in
point, as we lay on the bed, my loving wife pointed out to
Aliah that Daddy had a big head. Aliah came to my rescue
(I thought) by saying, "NO! Daddy's head not big ..." Ah,
the love of my two-year-old, already defending her dad. "...
it's huge," she concluded. With those words, she deflated
my over-inflated ego, which may be contributing to this
enormous head problem. Of course Mommy and Aliah
roared with laughter, Aliah not so aware of the context of
her description of me, but more caught up in the reaction
from Mommy. Don't worry about me; I've recovered, and
the counseling is sure to help me cope.

Aliah's perspective is a lot like our perspective on life,
isn't it? To some people my head is average, to others it's

8

big, and yet to some it's huge. What about those problems, or challenges, or tests, or questions, or coworkers, or car troubles, or bills, or ... whatever? When you look at them, are they normal? Are they average? Are they big? Or are they huge? Keep in mind it's all a matter of perspective. There is nothing in your life that you can't overcome: no obstacle too tall, no mountain too wide, no valley too deep, no bill too huge, no quarrel too heated. Remember Paul's words in his letter to the Philippian church? No? Oh, well let me remind you then. *"I know what it is to be in need and I know what it is to have plenty. I have learned the secret of being content in any and every situation, whether well fed or hungry, whether living in plenty or in want. I can do everything through him who gives me strength"* (Philippians 4:12-13). What's enormous to us is miniscule to God; He can overcome anything.

As a teenager I had the opportunity on two occasions to travel to Guyana, South America. It's a country popularized by the notorious Jim Jones cult. In a land of abject poverty and overwhelming desperation, my heart was gripped by the attitude of these people toward their plight. On one of these trips, two pastors met us at the airport to drive us to a remote village on the east bank of the Demerara River where we would be ministering. As we pulled into the driveway of the house where we would be spending the night, one of the tires on the car blew out. A family in a remote village with little or no income, struggling to survive in an economically depressed country, they had reason to be concerned, upset, angry or frustrated. Yet in that moment, their perspective of who God is and how He cares for and watches over us never shifted. As that dilapidated car hobbled on three wheels to a halt, the pastor who owned the car stared into the pampered eyes of these Canadian missionaries and exclaimed, "Just in time!" What perspective in an intolerable situation.

Later that night we walked to the crusade, which was already in progress. As we approached a church that had a dirt floor and thatched walls, a song floated across the night air, carried by the gentle breeze. The breeze was refreshing as it cooled the beads of sweat collecting on our perspiring bodies, but not as refreshing as the words of hundreds of impoverished Guyanese people that swept across our perspiring souls. "We're blessed; we're blessed; we're blessed; we are blessed. We've got shelter clothing and strength. We are blessed. We're blessed; we're blessed; we're blessed; we are blessed. We don't deserve it but yet we are blessed."

What has established your perspective for the situation that you face? Is it your lack of faith or frustration or doubt? If we build our perspective from the premise that there is nothing that we face that we can't overcome through a great God who is all powerful and who gives us all that we need and the strength for daily living, that which seems huge becomes a grain of sand on the shores of our life!

Chapter 3

SHE'D LOVE TOBOGGANING
BUT I HATE WINTER!

I LOVE WHITE CHRISTMASES, BUT I HATE WINTER. I love how beautiful houses look adorned with colourful lights glistening in the snow, but I hate winter. I wanted to take my two-year-old tobogganing for the first time in her life, mostly for my benefit, not hers, but I hate winter.

I have fond memories of my childhood: building snow forts and snowmen (or snow people—to be politically correct) and throwing snowballs at my siblings, but I hate winter. I remember the awesome feeling of coming inside on a cold winter's day, peeling off the constraining layers of snow pants and parka, and sitting next to an old gas stove to warm up while Mom made hot chocolate, but I hate winter.

Ever since I've joined the ranks of homeowners, I've dreamed of putting my creative hand to the task of decorating my own house with a *Griswold*[1] sort of light display that would attract tourists from all over, but I hate winter.

I was reminded of how much I hate winter, and heights, just the other day. While rummaging through our crawlspace, my loving wife found a bag of exterior Christmas lights that both of us had forgotten we purchased during the chaos of Boxing Day sales the previous year. My enthusiasm to create the most spectacular light display quickly waned as I stepped out in the sub-zero weather to install this newly recovered treasure. I'm sure it was almost Norman Rockwell as I positioned the ladder against the gable end of my roof and began attaching the string of lights to the eavestrough. OK, so maybe not Norman Rockwell, more like a Charlie Brown comic strip. Picture it: a slightly overweight (yeah, slightly) and balding man on an extension ladder literally shaking, mostly from fear of heights, not so much from the frigid wind blowing. By the time the job was done, 50 feet of Christmas lights hung securely fastened to the house, while the other 100 feet remained in their boxes, but for me the job was finished. I wandered back into the house reminded of one thing ... I hate winter!

"So what?" you say. So what? Perhaps my outlook on winter is the same outlook you have on life. Maybe you've become so cynical that you don't even give it a chance. After all, what has winter ever done to me? What reason do I have to hate such a perfectly normal season? What reason do you have for hating what you hate? Before you answer that, we must identify what it is that you actually hate. But even before we get there, let's reformulate the question. For many people, hate is too strong of a word, even when the emotion that we feel could be adequately described as such. So for the sake of argument, let's use this phraseology: "What do you dislike?" Is it your boss, your spouse, your friends, your banker, your neighbour, your house, your car, or your job? Now that you've identified what you hate, or dislike, I'll ask the question again. What reason do you have for hating what you hate?

When I consider what I hate, I realize that it's actually not the season that I hate. It's the shoveling, the mess and the bundling up. Or maybe, if truth be told, my hatred, or extreme dislike, for winter stems from a terrifying moment on Highway 2 one winter when I was sixteen years old. In the days when you could conceivably get your drivers' license on your sixteenth birthday, it wasn't too long before I had mine and was anxious to drive everywhere we went. My mom and I were traveling to London, Ontario to pick up my oldest brother from university. It was my first attempt to drive any distance in a developing snowstorm. The wind was blowing the weightless snow all over the road. The windshield wipers on our old Chevette were freezing to the window, disabling us from clearing the slush and snow, being sprayed by passing vehicles, from our windshield. I came over a hill and noticed a large snowdrift in front of our compact car. The drift stretched from the shoulder on our side of the road to the shoulder on the opposing side. In a split second, that tiny vehicle spun two or three times and landed axle high in the ditch.

Maybe you're like me in some ways. Your situation has spun out of control. It's a perfectly normal situation, something you do every day, something a lot of people do every day, but one dreaded day your world spins violently out of control, lodging you in a ditch with no seeming escape, and so forever you hate whatever it is you seem to hate.

As we journey through life, there are many things and many people that will make us guarded or trusting, happy or sad, thankful or ungrateful, stressed or relaxed, among other emotions. If you will strive to change your outlook on people, situations and seasons you will discover renewed hope and passion for the everyday. Drop the complacency of your pilgrimage and as Paul says, "Run the race with expectation of what's in store, uninfluenced by what's around us" (1 Corinthians 9:24 *paraphrase mine*). Life is not about summer, winter, spring or fall. It's not about being axle high in a snow-filled ditch. Life's not about whom we are or what we do. Life has meaning; we have purpose. We are His. Let's not be disillusioned by the superfluous. Instead, let's focus our energy on what counts: HIM, and everything else will fall into perspective.

Chapter 4

HER DEVELOPING VOCABULARY
GOD'S SILENCE

I F THERE'S ONE THING IN LIFE THAT I TRULY LOVE, it's being a dad. It's fascinating to watch, and to listen, as a world of discovery is revealed to my children. The most interesting part is watching my eldest grasp new ideas and concepts and listening as she translates her thoughts into words. Regularly, before bed, she and I will read a book, or concoct a story from the day's events, and then we pray. During one of these special moments I tried the unthinkable. I put my arm around her as we lay on my bed reading a story. In a split second she was on her knees, face to face, objecting, "Don't do that!" I kindly asked her not to talk to me that way, to which she responded, "Don't worry about it, Dad."

Words are important. Words carry information, express emotion, paint portraits of our dreams, envelope our worries, and build us up. On the other hand, they can also bring worry, fear, frustration, or they can tear us down. Spoken words are very important to us but probably not as important as the unspoken words.

When we communicate verbally with one another, we know each other's thoughts, motives and intentions precisely by what is said. When words aren't spoken, we are left to guess or deduce our own conclusions regarding situations, decisions and thoughts.

This is especially evident when God seems to be silent in our lives. You know what I'm talking about. You've been there before, or maybe you're there right now. You have a decision to make, and you want God to speak, to give you a sign, to send a word, but He seems to be silent.

This very thing has happened to me before. In my wisdom, I had come up with a plan to be debt free by selling the house that our family lived in to buy a cheap fixer-upper around the corner. When I shared the brainwave with my wife, the first words out of her mouth were, "Is this what God wants for us?" I knew immediately what she thought about the plan. Without saying it, I knew she would not consent unless God had first spoken it to me and subsequently confirmed it in her spirit. This has been our method of operation since we were first married. So when it comes to important decisions, we both know that we won't move until God moves us, metaphorically speaking. Anxious to explore the potential of this house, I set up an appointment with the real estate agent and began to pray for God to confirm in my wife what I hoped to be right.

It's funny how a simple time and date conversation can get messed up. Wednesday at 10:00 a.m., what's so hard about that? I arrived at the predetermined time, but to my dismay the real estate agent had misunderstood our conversation. I called his office and was disappointed to find that he was out. However, the kind receptionist agreed to send another agent over immediately. While I waited, I walked around the yard and peered through the windows. I even began to envision the house with new siding, a new deck, new windows, landscaping and much more. I'm a visionary; that's what I do.

While I waited impatiently, something on the front sidewalk caught my eye. Could it be? Was it true? Was this a sign from God? Was this His word to me, the confirmation I wanted, and my wife needed? Carved in the concrete sidewalk in bold letters was my name, "HOLMES". I was flabbergasted. How did this get there? Why would my name be in the sidewalk?

Based on this newly revealed "sign", when the real estate agent finally arrived, I walked with interest through the house, yet room by room, my enthusiasm quickly subsided as I realized that this house was not at all suitable for my small family, improvements or not.

Sometimes we look so desperately for a sign or a word that we overlook the obvious. I could have decided that my name in the sidewalk was a divine sign or look at the reality of the situation, that the house was unsuitable. Too often we attribute fleshly coincidences to spiritual encounters. I don't doubt that God cares for and loves each of us and at times allows things and situations to alter our course, but I also firmly believe that not every word or sign originates from Him.

Don't be deceived by misleading words or signs. Seek the truth in all that you do. Satan will try to mislead you, to sway you from the path that God intends for you. Don't be fooled, seek truth, trust God, and stick to His plan for your life. This means that you will need to be sensitive to His Holy Spirit. A few years ago, God sent a man into my life whose ministry was a blessing. As he ministered in our church, he taught me something very valuable that I live by to this day. If you believe God is speaking to you, or if someone shares a word with you that is believed to be from

God, it must be confirmed and checked with the Word of God, He will never contradict Himself or His Word.

Incidentally, I discovered later that the reason why my name was etched into that sidewalk was because the vendor's last name was also Holmes.

Chapter 5

SHE LOVES SHOES

WALK A MILE IN MINE

P RESUMABLY WE'VE NEVER MET, so you don't know who I am. If that's true, you probably don't know what I like. It's unlikely that, even if you do know me, you know any of my habits, good or bad. You probably couldn't guess what makes me laugh; actually I laugh at pretty much anything. My wife says that I don't cry too much, but even when I do, I don't always know why. Do you want to know something about me? Do you want to crawl in the mind of the man who authored these words? Do you want a snapshot of one of my best kept secrets? The fact of the matter is that I like clothes? I like buying new clothes, I like wearing new clothes, and I even like shopping for clothes. Even as I write it, it kind of sounds feminine, doesn't it? Furthermore, I hate paying full price for clothes. I shop at discount stores and outlet malls. I rush to the clearance rack and go to secondhand stores when they have sales. I don't know what ever birthed this fetish in me, but I'm actually OK with it. So, now that you know I like clothes, but hate to spend a lot on them, let me tell you a story.

For years I coveted a pair of shoes. It wasn't that I didn't have shoes; it was that I wanted a pair of special shoes. No, they wouldn't make me run any faster or make me taller. I'd come to understand that these shoes were the most comfortable shoes ever made. These shoes would form to my feet and give me that cushioned walk that could make me feel as though I was walking on a cloud. Perhaps it was this unquenchable desire in me that started my daughter's fetish for shoes, too. Give her a closet full of shoes, and she's intrigued for hours. It doesn't matter if they're six inches too big; she parades them around our house, stumbling and bumping into things, but she loves her shoes.

The problem with the shoes that I wanted was the price tag. Even on sale, I could only find them around 100 dollars. Year after year my desire increased and my feet grew weary. Every time I needed a new pair of shoes, I searched for an opportunity to satisfy this yearning in my *sole* (now I'm just being dramatic). I could never bring myself to spend that kind of money on shoes.

I know by now you're almost in tears feeling sorry for me, and your heart is sympathetic to my predicament. But lift up your head, this tragic story has a ray of hope. The years of longing, the sleepless nights, the daily wanderings of my mind came to an end one Christmas morning as I tore through the glistening paper of a Christmas gift that had my name on it. In amazement and bewilderment, I found once and for all the special shoes—in my size, and best of all, I didn't have to pay for them. They were a gift. For the lay person that means they were free, an excellent benefit to any bargain hunter.

After guarding my new prize from the slush and snow and coating them not once, but twice in leather protector, I finally ventured outside, proudly wearing these long sought after shoes, excited about the inevitable comfort that they were sure to bring to my long aching feet. My fatal mistake was that the first time I wore them, my wife dropped me off at our church, leaving me to walk home.

I quickly learned on that treacherous night that the hype surrounding these over-priced shoes was false. Can you imagine a grown man walking home at 11:00 at night, almost in tears because of the excruciating pain being inflicted upon his helpless feet? It was laborious to move one foot in front of the other. I would have probably had more comfort walking barefoot on a bed of nails; the pain was intense.

You would have thought that I learned my lesson, but I didn't. Some call it stubborn; I call it committed. My family knows that it's just how headstrong the Holmes men can be. I was desperate for these prized shoes to be all to me that I expected them to be, so I wore them out the next day. Walking from the house to the car was painful, but I tried against all odds not to express this pain to my wife. Ultimately I had to admit defeat. These were the most uncomfortable shoes I had ever worn.

It's alright though; my old shoes were anticipating my return. When I opened the closet, I'm certain they smiled at me. They knew I'd come back. They knew the special shoes weren't half as comfortable as they were. They waited patiently for me and within two days, I had reinstated them to their former position as my favourite pair of shoes.

Have you ever longed for something? Have you ever thought to yourself, "If I could only have that"? Have you considered how much better your life would be if things were different? Remember Mary and Martha? Their brother Lazarus had died. If only Jesus would have shown up sooner. In their minds the opportunity for a miracle was lost. The opportunity to transform a desolate circumstance had been missed. If only Jesus had come at their first beckoning, the situation wouldn't have been as tragic as it was. Though the timing was different than Mary and Martha anticipated, Jesus did ultimately come. They desired to spare their dear brother from the tomb; Jesus desired to raise him out of the tomb. The mourners had already gathered by the time Jesus arrived, signifying that these sisters hadn't received what they longed for. Their dreams were shattered, their hopes dashed. How could anything good rise out of the misery of this situation now? Unbound by the natural, Jesus fulfilled the hearts' cry of these sisters; it just occurred differently than they expected.

Sometimes our hopes and dreams don't play out exactly how we wish they would. It doesn't mean that our desires are wrong or that our thoughts are misguided. It's just that we neglect to recognize that God's promise to us is that He will satisfy our desires with good things (Psalm 103:5). If He promises to do it, He will do it. His promise to Mary and Martha was that this situation would not end in death. However, though He promised death wasn't the end, Mary and Martha thought a tomb meant it was over for their brother. I believed that a pair of high priced shoes was the answer to my intense longing. Life isn't perfect or easy or exactly what we want when we want it. Sometimes what we get isn't even what we really set out looking for. Mary and Martha wanted a man healed; Jesus wanted the dead raised. The greater of the two was for the dead to come back to life, a crowning moment for Jesus by far. Sometimes our dreams have to die so that Christ can be glorified as He rebirths, or raises back to life, our heart's cry. Don't be fooled, like I was, by the false assumption that a high priced pair of shoes will give you a better walk or, like Mary and Martha, that a dead brother is the end of the story or that whatever you wish for will be the right answer. Jesus wants to demonstrate Himself through you, to produce a defining moment in your life. Our walk isn't always cushioned and padded or comfortable. Don't look for a high priced pair of shoes to make life better; just walk better in the shoes you have. Let God's spirit finish this for you!

Chapter 6

SHE LOVES TO PLAY

BUT IT'S ONLY 7:30 A.M.

I T WAS 7:30 A.M. (If you keep that in mind, you'll understand how my mind functions first thing in the morning.) Our alarm clock, that we fondly named Abbey when we got her ten months earlier, woke us as she does every morning at precisely the same time. She's not like a conventional alarm clock. There's no annoying buzz, just a faint whimper in the distance. I wouldn't say it's soothing, but it's definitely less irritating than the drone of most alarm clocks. Unlike on many clocks, the snooze button isn't actually a button, but a well placed soother that tends to give us about another hour of sleep before the piercing final cry. Most clocks today give you a measly nine minutes. As you can imagine, this method of waking is not dependable. Just the day you actually want to wake at 7:30 a.m., your ten-month-old is bound to sleep until 9:00 a.m. It's a fun little game in the world of parenthood. However, this early morning event has prompted some of the best social times for Aliah and me. I dutifully wake up, plug the soother into Abbey's mouth, turn and pick Aliah up, who is already recounting all of the things I promised to do with her that day. We head for the kitchen. She perches on her chair while I pour cereal and milk for myself and boil the kettle for her morning oatmeal.

On this particular morning, she shapes her oatmeal into what she believed looked like a birdie's nest. While I vigorously eat my cereal, recognizing that I have limited time before I have to head to the office, she meticulously and methodically continues to sculpt her oatmeal. Once complete, an imaginary bird, affectionately named after Uncle Jeff and Aunt Vicki's dog Cosmo, arrives. Trying to play her little game, I welcome the bird with a cheery hi for which I'm scolded. "Birdies can't talk, Dad!" she reminds me. What was I thinking? I finally evoke enough encouragement, and she finishes her breakfast. We clear the table and rush down the stairs for her morning dose of cartoons. As I'm flipping through the channels, I see a commercial that I and the rest of the world have seen a hundred times. I'm 16 minutes into my day, and it happened: an epiphany of sorts.

Remember it was early, so this made a great deal of sense to me when I wrote it. Hopefully something tangible comes from it for you as you read it—presumably already alert. As I write this, all of the struggling domestic automakers are offering huge discounts and savings to entice buyers. Something once reserved for workers only, employee pricing, is now being offered to everyone. Some are even desperate enough to give away a computer with every automobile purchase. One automotive giant is trying to capitalize on their past successes by resurrecting an icon from the '80s. Do you know him? Lee Iacocca? In the '80s, he brought Chrysler into the forefront as the most innovative and zealous carmaker, positioning them to have a global impact on that industry. Under his leadership, Chrysler set industry standards and changed the way we look at and drive our cars. I'm not biased. I do drive a Dodge, but I also own a Chevy and have owned Mazdas and Toyotas, too. It's not so much the make that I care about as much as the price tag. Although this man once spearheaded changes and brought the automaker into a new era of car manufacturing, he's not leading the company. He's not forging new innovations. He's not rethinking the auto industry. In this century, he's a marketing tool.

Do you ever notice the church? Do you ever notice that it seems we are unsuccessful at reaching our market? Does it seem like the number of people buying into our "product" is decreasing every year? Does it seem harder and harder to move what used to be so easy to move? Maybe we (the church) need to change the face of our product. Maybe we need incentives. Maybe we need to make a bold move like Chrysler and bring back an icon to help us sell our product. Who would it be? Don't say Jesus. From a theological standpoint, if we believe in the Trinity (Father, Son and Holy Spirit) and if we also believe in the omnipresence of the same, then we can't say we need to "bring Jesus back" because He's always with us, and the power of the Holy Spirit dwells in all of us. So who would it be? Paul, Peter, John the Baptist or Stephen the Martyr? Who would help us fill our "showrooms" (sanctuaries)? Who could push Bible sales through the roof? Who would amass such a huge following that we'd have to build new production facilities (churches) where we could "build people", equipping them for the work of the ministry? (Ephesians 4:12)

This is where your marketing genius comes into play. If you're reading this—think hard. Who in the Bible could catapult the church of the twenty-first century into a new era of soul winning? Who would help us bring the Word of God to every corner of the globe and position us to reach millions in a short amount of time? Once you've determined for yourself who this "icon" would be, do a comparative study. Try to figure out what makes him different from you. What did he do that was so revolutionary? What inspired him to reach the lost?

Let's stop for a moment and consider the book of Acts. After all, if we are going to comment on, discuss or debate who or what the modern day church needs to be culturally relevant, Holy Spirit empowered, useful and effective for the twenty-first century church, we must use those records as our catalyst for conclusive arguments.

Throughout this book, Luke offers some compelling reflections on the power of the Holy Spirit, focusing predominantly on the life-changing, life-giving miracles that occurred through the ministry of the apostles. Unprecedented numbers were being added to the church, the dead were coming back to life, the lame were walking, the dumb were talking, and cowards were standing up with unparalleled boldness, preaching with conviction. I don't know about you, but if you're like me, that's what I long for. That's the desire of my heart. One of my favourite musical groups, Switchfoot, sings a song the words of which have become my personal anthem. "I want to see miracles, see the world changed ..."[2]

Those same words resonated through the countryside of Jerusalem, Galilee and Judea as the early church was scattered under the persecution of Saul and the Sanhedrin. There was nothing that seemed to limit these early converts in their ambition, and the Holy Spirit certainly matched their passion with power, demonstrated through signs and wonders.

So how do the Book of Acts, the miraculous signs and wonders and today's church have significance on the question that I posed to you earlier? What's the significance to you and me in the here and now?

As we contemplate the church in Canada, and experience what we term church in many different ways, it is apparent that church is many different things to many different people. To some it is reduced to an organizational body whose theological standpoints are as diverse as the number of ethnic groups in the world today, the chief distinctive of Christians being love and acceptance. Opposite to that viewpoint is the belief that Christians are extremists, bigots, closed-minded, shallow intellects, whose radical behaviour is repulsive. Somewhere in the mix, there is perhaps a morally-, ethically- and theologically-sound platform from which we can describe and understand better what church is and how we can effectively impact a nation with the power of God and stand for truth and love, just as Christ did.

If you're reading this, I'm making an assumption that you understand the allegory of the church as the "body of Christ". No doubt you've heard 1 Corinthians 12 recited frequently, reminding us that, though we are individuals and we are numerous, we are all one body collectively. Keeping Paul's analogy in mind, I'd like to propose to you a theory of what life in this body is like without the Holy Spirit empowering us. It's what I've dubbed the ALS Theory. I'm sure you've heard of Amyotrophic Lateral Sclerosis (ALS). Maybe you would more aptly recognize it as Lou Gehrig's disease. ALS is the most common form of motor neuron disease. It is a progressive, debilitating, usually fatal disease. Walking, speaking, eating, swallowing, breathing and other basic functions become more difficult with time. The voluntary muscles weaken and become immobile, leaving two to three Canadians dead every day from this disease.[3]

Paul made no mistake when he compared the church to a body. If you're alive, you know the inevitability of our bodies becoming sick or contracting illness. I'm sure you've experienced death (presumably not your own), so you know the frailty of the human body. Christians without the power of the Holy Spirit are the equivalent of a body with ALS. I liken empowerment of the Holy Spirit to the life and strength of a body of believers. By no means do I intend to belittle the disease or those who struggle or have passed away from its cruel affects, and I'm certainly not trying to portray the global church as a dying or lifeless church. I am, however, attempting to heighten our perception of the importance of being empowered by the Holy Spirit to fulfill the mandate given to us by Jesus Christ. The Holy Spirit to the early church was not a banner under which to carry out business. It was the power and authority of God, alive and working in that day in the lives of all who would believe. Twenty-first century Canada need be no different. The Holy Spirit is the lifeblood of the church (the body) that desires to change a nation, to change a community, to change a life. Without the Holy Spirit at work in and through us, we are suffering from a progressive and ultimately fatal disease, functioning as a body without strength. Like a human who suffers from ALS, a church that operates without the power of the Holy Spirit, just exists, unable to carry out normal functions, let alone achieve greatness.

In my lifetime, I've only met one person who is incapable of smelling. Although, most people I know have this ability, few I'm sure have ever smelled death like Peter would have when he entered the room where the corpse of Tabitha (Dorcas) lay (Acts 9:39). Into the poorly ventilated room, where numerous people had gathered to mourn, Peter entered. The air was thick; the stench was putrid. Many of us would have turned and ran. Some of us would have doubled over in the corner, tasting our last meal in reverse. But the smell of death didn't dissuade Peter. The smell of death reminded him of the power of the Holy Spirit, and he cleared the room, prayed to God, and ordered that lifeless body alive again.

I wonder which of our senses need to be heightened to invoke a passion in us to become the icon who will ultimately reach the lost and hurting in our world, in our nation, in our cities, or in our families. What do you need to see? What do you need to smell? What do you need to hear? What do you need to touch to motivate you to live it out in your life? Are you like me? Do you want to see miracles? Do you want to see the world changed? Do you believe that God is going to save the souls of your loved ones? Do you envision the blind seeing, the lame walking, and the deaf hearing? I'm not talking about a movement or an identity. It's not about being radical or charismatic. It's about doing what we've been commissioned by God to do. Very simply, go! (Matthew 28:19)

Can I propose to you that if you let the Holy Spirit work through you, you will become the revolution, an icon of truth, changing your world for Christ?

Chapter 7

SHE'S NOT THAT NAÏVE ANYMORE

DOUBLE OR NOTHING?

MORNINGS ARE GREAT, AREN'T THEY? The rising sun. The cool morning air. The dew glistening on the grass. The smiling face of the drive-thru worker at a local coffee shop. Most mornings go off without a hitch. But recently, as I pulled my van to this little window on the world, a gleaming face blurted, "One thirty-five." On such a rare day as this, I actually had the exact change and slipped it without incident into her tiny green hand. No, it wasn't actually green. I say green, because as she turned to the cash drawer, I noticed the words that every employee dreads to wear on their name tag, and every customer cringes at—"In Training".

After placing my change in the cash drawer, with a smile, she turned back to me and said, "One thirty-five."

In that split second, a million things raced through my mind. *How* odd. *Did she forget already that I paid her? Obviously training isn't going too well.* I finally blurted out through the hysteria of jumbled thoughts, "I—uh, just paid you."

As she handed me the coffee, she gave me a look. You know that cynical look you get when someone complies with your request, but you know deep down they don't completely believe you. It was as if she was thinking, *Yeah, right, if you say so* ... It's the same look I get from my two-year-old when I tell her that she can't do or have something, and without hesitating she asks, "Why?"

"Because I said so" doesn't cut it anymore, so I attempt to devise some philosophical reason why she must honour my request, but in her young, unadulterated mind she knows that I lack substantial reasoning, and she gives me that look. That's the same look I got from this "trainee". I wanted so desperately to open my door and plead with this woman to believe me, to ask her if she honestly thought I had just taken her for a free coffee. But as you know, in the drive-thru at 8:30 a.m., the only sensible thing to do is drive off. The brick wall would have never given way to my cheap metal door anyway. She wanted me to pay twice for something I hadn't even yet received.

I don't know if you follow baseball or if you remember the steroid controversy in 2005 with a player named Mike Morse. Personally I don't like sports too much. Even if I did, baseball certainly wouldn't be my favourite. Nonetheless, Mike Morse, shortstop for the Seattle Mariners, tested positive for steroid use and had been suspended for his third time for what he said all related back to the same incident two years prior. On national news he claimed that he had paid the price three times for one mistake. It sounds a lot like my childhood all over again. Being the youngest of four children, I paid the price for all the wrongs that my siblings caused, or at least it seemed to me that I did, so I can relate to someone who feels that they are unjustly punished. He went on to say that if anyone were charged for a crime, went to jail and were subsequently released, the authorities wouldn't come and pick that person up again, claiming that more time was required to pay for that same crime.

Every day we have is a gift. Every breath we breathe is a gift. Our freedom in Christ, freedom from the bondage of sin, was bought with a price, but we didn't have to pay for it. There is no High Commission continually recounting our failures and suspending us for past offences. There are no tellers waiting at a drive-thru window collecting tolls, and charging double for what has already been paid for. Yet, we live as though the price is great. We jack up the toll every day by worrying and fretting. I for one heap toll charges on myself. I tend to worry sometimes. I tend to try and work things out myself—and my wife glibly reminds me to trust God. Yes, I'm a pastor. Yes, I believe that God can work all things out. Yes, I've drilled congregants from the pulpit about this very issue. Yet I'm reminded again and again that I am, in fact, a man, a man of flesh, so when confronted with the question, "Double or Nothing?", I emphatically choose "Nothing!" Thank You, God, for paying my price. Thank You, God, for carrying me through.

Is your burden heavy today? If so, you're paying double for something that was already bought. Check between the covers of your leather file folder on those gold-lined pages. That purchase order is stashed away in there somewhere; I know it is. Check right around 1 Corinthians 6:20 "... *you were bought with a price* ..." The conclusion of that verse is actually my whole point. "... *therefore glorify God in your body, and in your spirit, which are God's.*" Because of the fact that we pay nothing, we must live as treasures of Him. Treasures of God? Treasures of the God who "owns the cattle on a thousand hills" (Psalms

50:10)? Treasures of the God who intricately formed the vast expanse of the farthest reaches of this universe? Treasures of the God who spoke light into existence and at the sound of whose voice, the elements obey? It seems unlikely, doesn't it, unlikely that this great and mighty, all-powerful, all-knowing King considers us His treasures? Consider what Paul teaches in his second letter to the Corinthian church. *"God who said let light shine out of darkness made his light shine in our hearts to give us the light of knowledge of the glory of God in the face of Christ. But we have this treasure in jars of clay to show that this all surpassing power is from God and not from us"* (2 Corinthians 4:6-7).

When it comes to God's power dwelling in us and His anointing empowering us, I'm thankful that it is by His own accomplishment on Calvary that I am entrusted, as a jar of clay, an earthen vessel, to carry this treasure. When life is complicated, remember you're not a debt or a liability; you're a treasure of the King!

Chapter 8

I LOVE HER THE MOST

GOD LOVES ME THE MOST

THE BLANKET STILL STRETCHED from the coffee table to the back of the chair, reminiscent of the previous day's adventures with my two daughters. In our house, we've designated one room as a toy room to accommodate their collection of birthday, Christmas and "just because" presents that their grandparents have spoiled them with. This room is a children's paradise. I certainly never had anything like it in my childhood. With a quick glance, you would notice two tents, a bike, a bin full of toys, a child size table and chairs for colouring, and a box full of dolls and teddy bears. Regardless of all of this, their biggest thrill is a haphazardly placed blanket that fortifies the corner of a room, or the space between a couch and table, forming a makeshift hut. It's about the easiest and cheapest form of entertainment for these two fun-loving girls. Even after they go to bed, I often find myself in the toy room on my own. No, not playing. I'm well beyond that in my years, though my wife might tell you my maturity doesn't equal my age. I go in to clean up. That's my job. The girls go to bed, leaving the toy room a mess, and usually each morning it has mysteriously cleaned itself, every toy in the right bin, every book on its shelf, and the bike neatly tucked into a corner. I don't know if the girls ever realize that this room is neat. They never ask, and I never tell them. It just happens. As I clean up, I reminisce of Abbey, my one-year-old, laughing and giggling. She talks in baby gibberish that I don't even pretend to understand. But I respond to her by whispering in her ear, "I love you the most, Abbey!" She giggles more, mostly because my breath tickles her neck.

You might think it odd that out of my two daughters, I tell the youngest that I love her the most. You may even become indignant thinking, *How could anyone love one child more than* the *other?* Before you write me off as an uncompassionate, negligent father, let me shed some light on your incredulous thoughts about me. After playing in our makeshift tent, and after brushing our teeth, and after putting on our pajamas, my eldest, Aliah, climbs into bed. She sheepishly recites the same prayer that she's said ever since she's been old enough to talk. It goes like this, "Thank you for Mommy and Daddy and Abbey and me. Thank you for Hannah and Avery. Thank you for Nana and Papa and Grandma and Grandpa. We love you Jesus, a-men." Predictably, she then turns and asks me, "Was that a good prayer?"

"Yes, Aliah, that was a really good prayer," I encourage. Then I swiftly lean in and her long curly hair tickles my nose, but I don't stop. I press in until my lips touch her ear and I whisper, "I love you the most!"

For her it's a cue to begin an endless banter with Dad. "No, I love you the most!" she replies. This dialogue continues for a few minutes until she finally says, "Do you know how much I love you?"

I already know the answer, but I play dumb and ask, "How much?" Stretching her tiny arms out to her sides, as far as she can, she says, "This much!" Then we giggle and embrace; she drifts off to sleep, and I anxiously await our next rendezvous.

I imagine that's what God does with us. As we laugh and play, or mourn and cry, or when we're just living oblivious to His presence in our lives, He gently calls to us, "I love you the most!" Our pompous attitude sometimes causes us to grow indignant if we ever feel like He really does love someone else more than us. But the reality is that, only minutes ago, it was to you that He was whispering, "I love you the most." Love is not completely depletive. There's no maximum on it. There's no limit, and it doesn't get overdrawn. I have as much love for Aliah as I do for Abbey. It doesn't mean that each gets 50 percent. By that logic, being the youngest of four children, I would have only been loved 25 percent—or less if you consider my parents' love for one another. Though it seemed at times, in my immature, childish mind, that I was under-loved, I know now that my parents loved me and continue to love me 100 percent, just as I do my daughters and my wife. If that philosophy is true of our human love toward one another, how much more true must it be of our Heavenly Father's love for us? Are you stumped? Maybe Paul's words can help you answer this question. *"But God demonstrates his own love for us in this: While we were still sinners, Christ died for us"* (Romans 5:8). Do you see the parallel between God's treatment of us and my treatment of my daughters?

In loving all sinners, and sending His Son to Calvary for all, He very much asserts Himself to a large degree in the same way I did to my beautiful girls. Each thrust of the mallet as it struck the nails, piercing his flesh, beat out the words, "I love you the most!" And it was spoken to me.

Each bead of blood that dripped from the thorns protruding into his tender scalp cried, "I love you the most!" And it was spoken to you. Every bruise on his body called, "I love you the most!" And it was spoken to your unlovable neighbour. Each gash on His back screamed, "I love you the most!" And the world gazes unaware. It was spoken to them!

How do you respond when you know that you are loved? Does it make you happy? Do you respond in love? I think so. So live loved!

Chapter 9

HER SAFETY EQUIPMENT

MY BODY ARMOUR

M AYBE IT WAS THE FACT THAT SHE JUST TOLD me that I had no hair or maybe it was the unseasonably warm weather we were experiencing. Whatever the reason, perhaps a culmination of the two, I knew it was time to get out of the house. The cherished bike she had received from Santa Claus was sure to be the distraction to shift her attention away from the television, where it had been fixed for the past three months, to the great outdoors.

Don't be bothered; I know Santa isn't real and so does she, but no matter how much I remind her that Mommy and Daddy bought her the bike, she's convinced that Santa brought it—no harm done as far as I'm concerned.

I was excited to finally be breathing fresh air as we stepped out the front door. After being trapped inside for the previous three months of winter, I'm sure the couch was relieved too. If it were an animate object, it would have been trying to reshape itself instead of prominently displaying the imprint of my figure. Remember I hate winter, so through this cold snap, I had become "close" with my couch. Aliah was as excited about being outside as I was. This new pink bike, trimmed with streamers and a backpack, was highly admired by this little girl.

She climbed on the bike, and we began our journey down the driveway and up the road to the corner, where we circled back to do a loop in our cul-de-sac. As she peddled, I walked beside her, not really doing anything—except giving her confidence, I suppose. In my wisdom, I decided to let her try going up the road on her own. This inexperienced decision soon turned tragic. Innocently I deducted that since the training wheels were functioning properly, keeping her upright, and she was wearing a fitted helmet, she would be safe. However, when she realized I wasn't walking in her shadow anymore, she began to fear. I don't know at that young age what causes us to fear something that we haven't yet experienced, but somehow she knew that danger awaited her. Without ever having done it before, she understood that at any moment this bike could spill, and she would become one with the asphalt. Without ever feeling the sting of gravel embedded in her tiny hands or tasting the salted roadway, fear of all those things gripped her. At that moment, her fear became a reality as she attempted to realign me in her sight. With one swift motion she turned her head to see me, and her hands, which firmly gripped the handlebars, followed causing the tiny pink bike, traveling at top speed for her, to fall over because of the sharp turn.

Have you ever had a bad fall off a bike? I did. I was about eight years old. It's one of the many vivid memories I have as a child. It was the age that lacked safety devices. We didn't need car seats, or seatbelts for that matter. Neither were we required by law to wear a safety helmet while on our bikes. It makes me wonder how we ever made it through life with so little protection. It's almost as if there was some higher power looking over us—protecting us, caring for us, but that's another story. During the summer, while school was out, my parents were constructing an addition on their home, which is inconsequential to this story, except that it explains why my grandfather was at my house early one morning.

It was early, as I stated, my brother and I were anxious to play as boys are. I remember getting on our matching matte black BMX bikes and heading down Book Street. That's where the vividness stops. Everything after that never resurfaced in my recollection. To this day I believe what happened was that, in my excitement to play, I awoke too early and fell asleep at the handlebars. I didn't regain consciousness until I was home again in the bathroom, where my mom was cleaning the wounds on my hands and face. This was probably one time that a safety device such as a helmet would have been warranted. The scab on my face could have made me the poster child for bicycle safety week. Picture my mangled face with the words, "Don't Let This Happen to You!" scribed across the bottom. In that tiny bathroom, I became coherent, yet unaware of what had happened and oblivious to the extent of my injuries. When I asked how I got there, Mom told me that my grandfather had carried me back to the house. For some reason, in my unconscious state, I wouldn't let my brother touch me. Only the kind, gentle hands of my grandfather were suitable to carry my fragile body back home. Thankfully my injuries were minor, and I fully recovered with no permanent scaring, although I did have to spend one night in the hospital, my only hospital stay to date.

It's painful. Falling off of a bike, I mean. If it's happened to you, you know the feeling. Do you know what else is painful? It's when you realize that your focus is no longer on God, that He's not in your shadow, and you're not in His. Based on our understanding of God, and the truth of Scripture, we know that God never leaves us (Joshua 1:5; Deuteronomy 31:6). Though I wasn't in Aliah's line of sight, I was watching her. I was close. I knew she was safe. It's the same in our lives. God is never too far from us to catch us when we fall. And like the helmet and training wheels on Aliah's head and bike, He gives us safety equipment too and implores us to suit up every day.

> *"Therefore put on the full armor of God, so that when the day of evil comes, you may be able to stand your ground, and after you have done everything, to stand. Stand firm then, with the belt of truth buckled around your waist, with the breastplate of righteousness in place, and with your feet fitted with the readiness that comes from the gospel of peace. In addition to all this, take up the shield of faith, with which you can extinguish all the flaming arrows of the evil one. Take the helmet of salvation and the sword of the Spirit, which is the word of God. And pray in the Spirit on all occasions with all kinds of prayers and requests. With this in mind, be alert and always keep on praying for all the saints"* (Ephesians 6:13-18).

With this in mind, don't let fear shift your attention from the fact that you are protected. When you feel like He's distant, He's not. His eyes and attention are focused unrelentingly on you. He is your strength. He is your defender. Walk uprightly, trusting fully in Him.

Chapter 10

I'M A GREAT TEAM

BUT THERE IS NO "I" IN TEAM

I T WAS GRADE THREE, AND I SOMEHOW found myself playing soccer for the school team, at least for one game. It's odd that I even played because I'm sure I never tried out. All I can assume is that the team was short a player and didn't want to forfeit the game, so they called yours truly to play. I'm sure it wasn't because the coach watched me on the playground at recess dribbling the soccer ball down the field like an Italian pro. I'm sure that I was drafted out of sheer desperation. I don't know if we won or lost that game, though the latter seems most likely. What I do remember is that I was disappointed about the fact that I couldn't keep the jersey. I thought having a jersey would at least portray an image that I was some kind of athlete, but even the dream of imitating an athlete was illusive. This particular game was a home game, and though I wasn't a starting player, I did take to the field ... once. I'm not even really sure if I ran in the right direction during the game. I'm positive I didn't score, and I'm confident that the only part of my game that had any semblance of me knowing what I was doing was the fact that I followed the mass of little bodies chasing a black and white hexagonal patterned ball up and down the field. I remember the coach, Mr. Berelli, telling me what position to play as I ran onto the field, although I don't remember the position. It's as irrelevant now as it was then, considering I still don't know what any of the positions are.

So I was never an all-star or an athlete, and despite the fact that I had one day in the spotlight, so to speak, it never catapulted me into a soccer career. Until recently I never even cared much for sports of any kind. I had no desire to play sports, no desire to attend a sporting event with thousands of passionate fans, and no desire to sit in the comfort of my living room and watch sports on television. Lately, though, I've become fond of football, but even at that, I'm ignorant of what's happening. My appreciation for the sport is more of a desire to rest on the couch on a Sunday afternoon than it is a love or obsession for the game. Even now, when people ask me if I watch football I tend to lie and answer, "No." That way they don't try to engage me in any factual discussion about athletes or a sport that I know nothing about.

Regardless of your passion or your knowledge of sports, or your lack thereof, we do have something in common. In fact, all I really know about sports, you know, too. Actually, everyone on this planet knows what I know. Men, women, boys and girls, no matter how athletic or pathetic (like me), we all know at least one thing; it's the over indulged cliché, "There is no 'I' in TEAM!"

While that is a factual statement regarding the spelling of the word, the idiom is also very pragmatic when we consider our own existence and accomplishments. As a father, I've determined to make ready my daughter for the world around her. If she wants to sing, I'll enable her to take vocal lessons. Should she desire to skate, I'm sure I can scrounge enough cash to buy her first pair of ice skates. If she's at all interested in following her dad's noble steps onto the soccer field, she's already ahead of the game. At least one step ahead of where I was when I made my simultaneous debut and finale on the soccer field.

Together, she and I have broken all the traditional "not in the house" rules. We throw things in the formal living room. We have toys upstairs, downstairs, magnetically attached to our appliances and everywhere else in between, and we regularly push the furniture to ends of the room to play arena soccer in our living room. OK, so it's not really arena soccer, considering our living room is 12 feet by 16 feet in size. But it is indoor soccer nonetheless.

I'm not really sure if I make a good coach, being so uneducated in the sport, but to my daughter, I at least make a great net as she kicks the ball repeatedly between my legs, each time screaming, "Goooooo-al," followed by cheers and a high five. In this game of one-on-one, as if all eleven players were on the field passing, dribbling and shooting, she retreats to her side of the room without fail and smugly says, "I'm a great team!"

In her youthfulness, my daughter has yet to grasp the concept that one person doesn't constitute a team. The fact of the matter is that you and I as adults also tend to be unable to grasp that concept in our everyday lives. It seems simple, doesn't it? I don't mean the spelling; I mean the philosophical application that it has in our lives. Perhaps even harder to understand is its implication in our spiritual lives. Think about it; we push and pull, worry and fret, manipulate and pledge and negotiate, all the while trying to move the hand of God to operate exactly how we want, when we want. We want Him to follow the exact path of motion that we foresee as "divine" so that at the end of a long, hard day we can run around and chant, "I'm a great team!" That attitude certainly isn't demonstrated to us in the life of Jesus Christ. I mean, here He is, being fully God incarnate, yet by very nature, a human. Of any human being ever to walk the face of the earth, only Jesus could have made "I'm a great team!" his personal slogan. Yet, throughout Scripture, in His humility, He demonstrates His need for God the Father. Similarly, His disciples certainly didn't exhibit an "I'm a great team" approach to ministry. They recognized their need and dependency on each other, and more importantly, their need for God and His Holy Spirit. If you read through the book of Acts and note the major advances that the early Christians were making in terms of personal growth, numerical growth and spiritual growth, three things we hopefully strive for every day ourselves, it was preceded with "team" prayer. They met together and prayed together and waited together. The Holy Spirit bore witness to them, and it was everything but an "I" mindset.

What does your life resemble at this point in time? Are you like a squad of children who are newly introduced to the game of soccer? In their little minds, there are two things on that field that are important: the ball and themselves. If they don't get the ball, they're frustrated and usually run off the field to their parents, crying, claiming it's unfair. Sounds a lot like us at times, doesn't it? Life's not fair. The problems are too great. Everyone else has what we want and, no matter how fast we run, we can't seem to catch up, or by the time we do, that which we've chased so hard is now going in a completely different direction. So we run off the field agitated and advise our Father how unjust the whole game of life is. And He lovingly reminds us what our position is, why we don't need to always have control of the ball, and how important we are in the bigger "team" picture. Then He gently places

His hand on our shoulder and slowly repositions our focus back on the field. In His gentleness, we didn't even recognize that with His other hand He had wiped away our tears. The only indication is that our once moist eyes are now dry. Then with a loving nudge that only He can give, He encourages us to re-enter the game. He recognizes our apprehension, so He caringly crouches, positioning His lips next to our ear, close enough that we feel the warmth of His breathe on our neck while the warmth of His words sweep over our souls, "There is no 'I' in team!" With that, we're back in the game. The score board is even, the ball in our possession, and our focus is on the team, not ourselves. Finally the game of life seems just and fair, and we recognize our need and our dependency on the team.

SHE THINKS I'M PRICELESS

SO DOES GOD

THE "ANTIQUES ROADSHOW" HAS BECOME a very popular television program that debuted on PBS in 1996 in the UK. The premise of the show is that individuals bring artifacts and family heirlooms that have been passed down from generation to generation and things they've collected at yard sales to someone educated in antiquities. These appraisers examine and survey the assets as the owner watches and listens to a dissertation about the origin and history of these uncovered trophies in the hopes that the appraiser will declare that what they've brought is a priceless treasure. The reason that most viewers are fascinated by this show is because of the innate longing in every human being for unearned, undeserved wealth. Often the story unfolds something like, "I bought it at a yard sale for 25 cents ten years ago and recently uncovered it in my attic while I was cleaning it out." Then the host reveals that this yard sale junk is actually a costly relic. The most amazing part of this show is the obscure places that individuals find items of great value. Some find them in their attics, others in the walls of their home during a renovation project. Some have had them handed down to them from previous generations, while others bought them for pennies at a yard sale. Regardless of where the treasure comes from, the fact is that items of great value don't always come from the most obvious places. When you think of a tea cup worth thousands of dollars, you assume that it is part of the China collection stored under lock and key in Windsor Castle or recovered from the bottom of the Atlantic, out of the ruins of the unsinkable Titanic. It's rare to think that something of great value ever comes out of the dirt and clutter of an attic or in the destruction of a wall during a renovation project, but that's precisely where things of true value seem to come from, don't they?

Speaking of a treasure that comes from dirt, I like to think of myself as a priceless treasure some days. Do you? It's not a derogatory statement nor does this sentiment have negative connotations. After all, we are made from the dust of the earth, right? Do you ever consider yourself to be a priceless treasure? My daughter thinks I am. How do I know, you ask. She told me. That's right; one afternoon after trying to convince her to have a nap for what seemed to be hours but in reality was only minutes, I found myself snuggled up in bed with her. I wasn't coerced; I was actually a bit tired myself and thought the nap would be good for both of us. Seconds passed as we lay perfectly still, but I knew it was the calm before the storm. If you now have, or ever have had children, you know that you can't lay down with them when they are obviously not tired and have an uninterrupted nap. So I knew the solitude was about to come to an end; I just didn't realize that I would be the assailant who broke the silence. Unintentionally, I sniffed her hair. It smelled flowery, suggestive of a rosebush I thought. She wasn't about to let me get away with this innocent maneuver though. Instantly she asked, "Did you just smell my hair?"

For a split second I was embarrassed, but for no real reason. There was really no harm in what I had done. I recognized that I didn't need to qualify my actions so I simply responded, "Yes."

"Why?" she snapped.

My response was sincere, "Because it smells pretty, like …"

Before I could finish my sentence she interrupted and said, "You're priceless, Daddy!" I laughed, she laughed, and the illusive nap had escaped us for another day.

I wasn't even sure if she knew what she meant. Can she truly grasp in her evolving mind what her words mean? Does she even fathom the depth of her wisdom at times? I don't think she does, but her words still raise some thought-provoking study, research, dialogue and commentary. I don't think she intended, with her words, to portray me as a priceless treasure, a father who she knew she could depend on, who loved and cared for her, who, in her mind, was irreplaceable. I think somehow in her overdeveloped sense of humour, she was just making a joke at her dad's expense.

Nonetheless, I prefer to think the former to be the case, which causes me to make an interesting observation about our relationship with our father. Normally that phrase causes us to think about our Heavenly Father, God. But for a moment, let's think about our biological father. Psychologists and statisticians have all sorts of facts and data that demonstrate the influence that a father has in the life of a child. For instance, when fathers are involved in their children's education, including attending school meetings and volunteering at school, children were more likely to get A's, enjoy school, and participate in extracurricular activities, and less likely to repeat a grade.[4] Additionally, children who live with both parents are more likely to finish high school, be economically self-sufficient, and to have a healthier lifestyle than their peers who grow up in a broken home.[5] Many of you reading this will say that your father never had any influence on you. "He's been gone most of my life. He's never called. He's never written. He just doesn't love me. My dad has no influence on me!" Well, you're actually wrong. In saying that, I'm not presuming that your father is a good man, and I don't want to assume he's an all bad man either. Whether your father has been a loving, caring, highly involved, strong, moral and ethical role model in your life, or if he's been completely absent, he has influenced who you are.

Based on the research that I've already conveyed to you, some of you already recognize the advantages that you have because of your father's involvement in your life. We become good, kind, caring, loving and passionate people just like our father. We resemble our father's morals and Christian character. Yet, others of us live under the weight of unforgiveness and bitterness. We read some of the facts that seemingly plague children of single moms or absent fathers. Let me point out that some of you lived with both parents, but your father was still absent in your life. For that, you resent your father. You feel that you have no role model. You redirect your anger and hatred toward others, especially those in authority over you, and it impacts your life on a daily basis whether you recognize it or not.

Take some time for me right now, actually not for me, but for yourself. Think about your father. Think about your relationship with him. Is he a priceless treasure, a father whom you depend on, who loves and cares for you, who, in your mind, is irreplaceable? If so, you are among a minority of people in the world today, and you really need to celebrate this blessing in your life, this priceless treasure. If not, then maybe you're harbouring bitterness or resentment that is diminishing your true worth. Regardless of your past, or your father's involvement or lack of involvement, whether you've ever met your dad or not, you can break free of the past and move into a new blessing in your own life. You are a priceless treasure. No matter what your past has been like, no matter what you see when you look in the mirror, no matter who your father is, or what you did last night that you're ashamed of, the God of this world has made His light to shine in you, a priceless treasure, buried in the attics of our hearts, waiting to be uncovered by you, to be put on display for the world to see the worth, the value, the awesomeness of your life.

SHE WANTS TO WATCH
THE FLOWERS GROW

I'M TOO IMPATIENT

THROUGH THE COURSE OF A DAY, our patience can be challenged in very simple ways. At least, if your personality is similar to mine, it can be. For instance, a quick stop at the bank turns into a torturous reading and re-reading of the familiar, but dreaded, "please wait here for the next available teller" sign. A visit to the doctor turns into hours in a "waiting room". It happens everywhere we go. We wait in traffic, or we wait in a drive-thru line, or we wait in the express line of the grocery store, whose title tends not to convey the reality of the situation. If there is one thing that I struggle with, spiritually speaking, it is waiting, and no doubt you may share that attribute with me. The fact of the matter is that I'm not perfect! (Now that you've picked yourself up off the floor, continue reading.) I'm an extremely impatient person, but God in His infinite sense of humour continually reminds me to wait on Him.

Imagine with me for a moment that I have just given you a pot, a bag of rich soil, a sachet of seeds, and a watering can with fresh water in it. Essentially you have all of the key ingredients to create something good, something nourishing and something life-giving, but you have to know where to start. All of these items on their own are quite insignificant. The pot, as lovely as it may be, depending on your imagination, only serves as a visual attraction and a vessel to hold dirt. The soil is messy and useless as it is. The seeds offer no nourishment or value until they mature, but it's impossible for them to reach maturity without other factors being present. As much as water is necessary for the human body, and as much as it is a life source for every living thing, if it only ever sits in a watering can, it is purposeless. Yet the simple truth, and a good principle for us to observe, is that even when the essentials are mixed together properly, they are still immature, unusable, undeveloped and fruitless. Even though all of the ingredients are right, the ingredients aren't all that is needed. There is an unseen element—waiting. This truth is applicable in our spiritual lives as well. Yet we treat our prayer life and our spiritual journey much like those ingredients. We believe that mixing prayer, godly counsel and fasting with Bible study and church attendance constitutes the perfect recipe to bring the blessing, response or answer that we expect from God.

Farmers know very well the lesson of waiting. They know that there is a time to plant and a time to harvest. It's not only a law of nature; it's the word of God. Ecclesiastes highlights, in the third chapter, that there is a time and season for everything: specifically relating to our topic, a time to plant and time to uproot (Ecclesiastes 3:2). If we apply this principle to farming, you don't need to be a farmer to know that you can't drive huge machinery onto the field to harvest at the first bud. The crop is useless and valueless, and the harvesting machinery would destroy the tiny sprouts.

Pregnant woman know the lesson of waiting very well, too. When that home pregnancy test alerts them to the possibility of parenthood, they don't rush to the nearest hospital and demand to deliver. It's premature. There is a time of waiting. As much as I hate to say it, and even more admit it, waiting is good—especially in our spiritual lives.

It's a theme that resounds over and over again throughout Scripture. David in his psalms wrote, "I lay my requests before you ... and *wait* in expectation" (Psalm 5:3) and later, "I waited patiently ... and the Lord answered" (Psalm 40:1). Isaiah said, "The Lord longs to be gracious with you ... blessed are those who *wait* for Him" (Isaiah 30:18). Jeremiah declared, "The Lord is my portion therefore I will *wait* for Him" (Lamentations 3:24). Micah said, "I will *wait* for God" (Micah 7:7). Paul said, "... do not lack any spiritual gift as you eagerly *wait* for our Lord, Jesus Christ to be revealed" (1 Corinthians 1:7). Throughout Scripture, not only are we implored to wait, we're called to wait patiently, to wait eagerly, and to wait expectantly.

I don't pretend to be knowledgeable when it comes to gardening, but as an obedient husband, when my wife asked for a garden in front of our house, I obliged and began doing as she requested. In hindsight I realized that the timing was off. It should have been obvious, but to an inexperienced gardener like myself, I paid no attention to the particularly hot and dry summer we were having. I tried earnestly to keep that little garden watered, to keep life flowing into the leaves of the plants, but as hard as I tried, admittedly, all three of the flowers that I had planted died. I know you're probably laughing uncontrollably right now. Wondering how three flowers could constitute a garden, but for me, it was obviously more than I could handle. Since the flowers were already dead, one day while I was cutting the grass, I took the weed eater and trimmed them right down to nothing. A few days later, Aliah and I were playing in the yard, and I noticed that one of the flowers that I had butchered with the weed eater was actually blossoming. So I drew it to Aliah's attention. She squatted in front of that plant and said, "Dad, let's watch it grow." I laughed because it's so innocent and naïve to think that you can actually sit and watch a flower grow, especially if you're two years old and packed full of energy. But days later, as I thought about her comment, God quickened my spirit and spoke to me saying, "That's the kind of waiting that I'm asking for from you."

Plant your seeds; make your requests known, and wait. When the buds push the soil back, and the answer is slow in coming, wait! When the stem begins to press upward toward the light of the sun, and the circumstances take a small turn, wait. When the storm comes and the rain clouds form overhead, wait. When you feel like you are absolutely tired of squatting and watching the never-ending process of this seed growing, wait! And you say, "Well, how long do I wait?" *Wait until it's ready.* There is no prescribed time. Some things grow faster than others, but no matter how long it takes, wait patiently, wait eagerly, and wait expectantly—and in due time, God will bring about what He intends for your life.

In Isaiah 40, Jacob and the nation of Israel highlight something for us that I believe is the primary reason that we find it so difficult to wait. We fool ourselves into believing that nobody knows what we're going through. We believe that our situation is unique, that no one has ever been in our predicament. Therefore, we feel no one, not even God, understands where we are. So naturally we can't wait but must conjure up an answer or manipulate a result for ourselves. In this passage of scripture, the children of Israel say in verse 27, "Our way is hidden from the Lord. Our situation escapes His notice." In essence they were saying, "Lord, you don't understand our situation."

But Isaiah responds with wisdom, a wisdom that transcends time and is not only applicable to the past, but applicable to your life, to your situation, right now. He said, "Do you not know? Have you not heard? Just *wait*..." This is his response in the King James Version. In the New International Version, we read the word *hope* in place of the word *wait*. The reason it is used interchangeably in these two translations is because the original Hebrew word actually means *to hope strongly, to trust, to wait for with expectancy*. When Isaiah says "wait on the Lord" or "hope in the Lord", he is referring to a sure expectancy. He's saying, "Become totally dependant on, rely on, look to, trust in—believe it's going to happen. Don't try to work it out on your own. Expect that God will do what He's promised to do and carry you through."

I want to assure you that waiting on God is nothing like waiting in a hospital emergency room. It's nothing like waiting for the next available teller. It's definitely nothing like a visit to your local grocery store, waiting in the slowest *express* lane ever. Waiting on God is not a chore, it's not a waste of time, nor is it a huge inconvenience. Waiting on God is a necessary step in seeing the fullness of God revealed in your life. Plant your seeds, make your request known, and watch it grow. Watch the dreams and desires of your heart flourish into a sustainable, life-giving fruit. Watch the flowers of your life blossom into something magnificent.

God desires to do amazing things in your life. Some of you reading this feel physically, emotionally or spiritually empty. Others are struggling with sickness and disease.

Still others of you have been carrying around the same burden for years. Today is your day to be set free. Your brokenness will be mended! Today the seeds of healing have been planted in your fragile body. The emptiness in your life will be filled in the name of Jesus. And He will break down the walls of captivity. Wait with expectancy, wait eagerly, wait patiently on Him, and see what He can and will do in your life.

Chapter 13

SHE LIKES TO HIDE

I KNOW HOW TO FIND HER

THE CURTAINS WERE QUIVERING, and a pair of size five feet protruded from underneath the floor-length drapes. The silent giggles were the ultimate revelation of the whereabouts of this hiding little girl. It's not that I don't like playing hide and seek; it's just that we were rushing around getting ready to head out for the day, and as I intently called for my two-year-old to come and get her shoes on, she called back, "Come and find me!" Although I wasn't in the mood and felt the pressure of time, like she never seems to recognize, it did make me chuckle. It's the same every time. She wants me to count while she hides. Whether it's her tiny mass quivering under the blankets on my bed or the flailing curtains or the giggling in the closet, like every other child, she's not good at hiding. My favourite part of hide and seek is that, if I call out to her, "Aliah, where are you?" she unequivocally gives away her secret place, by responding, "I'm in here!"

My daughter is not alone in her lack of hiding ability. There are two other people that stand out in my mind who were among the hiding-challenged throughout the world. Hiding deep in the shrubbery of the Garden of Eden were Adam and Eve. In their sin and shame, they did what all of us often attempt to do: run and hide. But we, like little children, are not very good at hiding. Or maybe it's that our Father is really good at finding. After all, are you really convinced that when God entered the Garden that He actually didn't know where Adam and Eve were? Or like me, when I call out to Aliah, "Where are you?" do you think He knew? I mean it must have been blatantly obvious. The leaves must have been trembling, just like the curtain that my daughter was hiding behind. Why were they hiding? Did they think that for all of eternity they could veil their disobedience from God? Did they think that the half-eaten fruit would decompose before the Lord saw it on the ground? Did they truly think that the God of the universe, who handcrafted the tree of life, wouldn't notice the empty stem where the fruit once hung?

What about you? Why do you try to hide? Why do you stop attending church or become distant from friends and family who you believe have it altogether? All of us, for many different reasons, try to conceal ourselves at one time or another. But did you know that everything we do is visible to our heavenly Father? Let's consider the Gospel of Matthew for a moment, specifically the sixth chapter. This portion of scripture is invigorating, considering the context and application for us today. But specifically I want to highlight something for you to consider.

In this passage, Jesus is teaching the premises of holiness, of living a life of obedience and total surrender. Holiness, obedience and total surrender were certainly deficient in the Garden of Eden. Here Jesus is giving three very specific commitments that Christians should follow, those being to pray, to fast and to give.

When we consider the parameters that encompass hiding, there are two distinct attributes to consider: the first being negative and the second being positive. Consider again Adam and Eve. They hid out of fear, realizing that they had sinned against God. We, too, attempt to hide ourselves from God. We mess up or do something that we regret. We fight with our spouse, fly off the handle at our children, fail morally, neglect our devotions, or feel completely dispassionate about our relationship with God, so we hide. We think if we can avoid church, avoid our pastor, avoid talking to our spouse about the problem, then everything will be fine, and we won't have to deal with it. But all we're doing is hiding; we're not solving anything.

Now consider what Matthew is declaring to us in his Gospel. Doing things in secret can also be very positive, spiritually speaking. It's not about hiding ourselves from God or trying to conceal any wrong, impure, or unjust motives in our heart. It's simply living a life solely for the purpose of pleasing and honouring God, not showing off for man or neighbours or friends or family. Jesus declares in Matthew 6:4 that when we give in secret, with pure motives, for the express purpose of pleasing God, what He sees in secret will be rewarded openly.

The implication from both of these texts for us is that no matter what is done in secret, or in hiding, it will be exposed. If we have sin that we attempt to hide, He will expose what is done in darkness and bring it to light. Yet if we do what is pleasing to him, that, too, He will bring to light, but in the context of a blessing.

When the secret parts of your life are exposed, what will be uncovered? Will it be a life of shame and defiance? Or will it be a life of good, holy, noble acts of kindness, a life expressed through generosity and selflessness? What must Adam and Eve have been thinking as they attempted to hide themselves from God? What are you thinking right now about what happened yesterday or last week or a few minutes ago? Don't run and hide. Don't bury yourself in the shrubbery of self-denial, hoping to never be discovered. It won't blow over, but it can be mended and forgiven. Step out of your hiding spot, and step into the light of Jesus Christ.

Chapter 14

AM I PRETTY?

UNEQUIVOCALLY, YES!

C ONSIDER THIS STATEMENT, "We blame the evolving pursuit of beauty on societal intolerances, claiming that we must measure up to a standard that the unseen 'they' set for us, yet fail to realize that it's not entirely society's liability, but rather an innate longing in all of us for exquisiteness."

Perplexing isn't it? After all, when we feel as though we're not good enough, or too slow, too tall, too small, too fat, too skinny, or like we have too much hair or not enough, our tendency is to blame others for inducing objectionable standards upon humanity that we inevitably could never live up to, producing our own feelings of inadequacy. While I do agree that society, media and corporate earth have cashed in on the pursuit for perfection, it's my steadfast belief that *they* didn't create it, and frankly attributing its creation to those industries is essentially the easy way out. It's considerably harder to admit that our flesh is warring with our spirit in the unrelenting battle of self-gratification versus spiritual fulfillment.

If society was totally to blame for this inferiority complex, which I'm not completely sure they are, why would a little girl who watches TV, totally oblivious to the latest fashion trends and, as yet, uninfluenced by her peers, ask, "Daddy, am I pretty? Of course, any loving, caring, compassionate father is going to respond as I did, "Yes, you're very pretty!" The excitement in my voice caused her to giggle and blush. It was the answer she had hoped for, and presumably expected, but yet it was as though she was surprised by my response. Why should she be surprised? I've never told her that she is ugly. I've never asked her to consider a new hairstyle or to use cover up. In the natural, I see no fault, no blemish, no flaw and no blunder. She's my princess. I fathered her. I prayed intently for her in the womb and sang to her through her mother's tummy. I smiled with delight at her arrival. I proudly displayed her to friends and family that celebrated her arrival. I roll with her on the floor to play and build pretend houses from blankets and drink imaginary tea from her little porcelain tea set. We set out on wild adventures as we fabricate make-believe stories at bedtime. I run to her side when she cries. Her laugh makes laughter well up in me. When she smiles, my heart melts. When I'm away from home, I hear her voice and long to hold her and whisper in her ear how much I love her. When this little girl asks, "Daddy, am I pretty?" should anything else rise from the depths of my soul?

Take some time for a moment, and go stand in front of a mirror. These pages will wait for you; go ahead. As you gaze in the mirror, consider what you see. What is your perception of that reflection? What do you see? Do you see genuine beauty? Is there more forehead than you would prefer? Is your nose reminiscent of the marionette turned boy fable? Maybe you've realized that what you see in the mirror is only flesh, so as you pondered the reflection you peered deeper. Perhaps you were staring at your soul, and

CHRONICLES OF A TWO YEAR OLD

you reflected on unanswered questions, disappointments, failures or broken promises.

When I consider the sincerity of my daughter's question, and the significance of the question that I posed to you, I recognize that both are fundamentally flawed. As beautiful as my daughter is, and as beautiful and complete as I'm sure you are, the questions "Am I pretty?" and "What do you see?" are unimportant in light of this question: "Who do you see?" It's not *what* that is important; it's *who*.

When you look at your child, who do you see? When you watch your spouse, who do you see? When you lock eyes with a homeless person, who do you really see? Those families next door, who are you looking at when you see them? Or better yet, that reflection in the mirror, whose face is staring back at you? From Genesis through to Revelation, we're reminded that we aren't impetuously designed. We're not a mistake. We're not by chance. We're not a random coming together of molecules and particles. We are by purpose, a creation of intelligent design. There's a saying that's been coined, the origin of which I'm unsure, but it's completely false. You've heard it and even used it, I'm sure. *When God made you, He broke the mould.* Men and women use it to express their heartfelt compassion for one another, the inference being, that their partner is unique and that no one else could ever compare to them. Sometimes the term is used cynically, meaning no one else would ever want to be like a certain person. However, the Bible tells us that all of us are created in the likeness of God (Genesis 1:26; James 3:9). That means every blemish, every spot, every mark, any perfection or imperfection as we interpret it, is a reflection of His handiwork. So look one more time in the mirror, again answering this question: Who do you see? When that yearning wells up inside of you to be something that you don't perceive yourself to be, or when you spot someone whose life you would rather live, recognize this: You are a beautiful creation, a self-portrait of the Creator, fearfully and wonderfully made (Psalm 139:14). No one on earth is better, more beautiful, more talented or more complete than you. With over six billion manufactured to date, everyone is cast from the same mould, in the same image, with the same care of the Creator. None are greater, and none are lesser.

With this perspective, we can move from self-rejection to self-acceptance, recognizing with increased appreciation and passion who we are in Christ. When we believe that we are His creation, not by chance, and not a random occurrence, only then can we reach our full potential. Likewise, only when we recognize that everyone around us shares that same attribute, of being in the likeness of God, can we operate with the same compassion that Jesus Christ operated with as he ministered to people of all classes, races and genders.

By this standard, without any influence of society, or prejudices derived from media, possibly without having ever met you, I could answer you in much the same way that I responded to my daughter. "Am I pretty?" "Unequivocally, yes! You resemble your Father who is perfect in every way!"

Chapter 15

I LOVE YOU, DADDY!

FACE TO FACE

IT HAPPENS EVERY MORNING WITHOUT FAIL. It can be annoying, but subtlety cute and welcomed at the same time. It starts with the sensation that there is a draft, but I quickly recognize it's her breath on my face. As I open my eyes, I become aware of her small body sprawled over top of mine, her weight unobtrusive. In a split second, her dark hazel eyes blink, and she quickly says, with her face pressed to mine, "I love you, Daddy." You're wondering why this would be annoying to anyone. Am I insensitive? Do I reel at the expression of love from a little girl to her daddy? Emphatically not! Did I mention that it's usually 6:30 a.m.? I would never trade it for the world. As much as I love my sleep and yearn for the years when I set my own schedule again, I know I will one day long for that little princess to sprawl herself on top of me, face to face, cheek to cheek, nose to nose, morning breath to morning breath, and whisper in the solemnness of the daybreak, "I love you, Daddy." The most significant part isn't the word that she speaks; it's the passion in her eyes as we gaze at each other.

After a long night alone in her room, she passionately seeks acceptance and affirmation. Though another hour on the clock would do my aging body good, I never chastise her for her relentless pursuit of affection. I don't reject her or send her heartbroken back to her own bed. I tell her I love her, slide her tiny body in between the bed sheets, and try unsuccessfully to catch some more sleep before the alarm clock buzzes.

Have you ever been face to face with anyone? For most of us, a face to face experience is intimidating. We value our "personal space", as it's been dubbed. We're afraid of having to smell the breath of other people, or maybe we fear being spat upon, or maybe we're afraid others will smell our breath. Whatever it is, face to face encounters are few and far between and reserved for intimate moments. One such moment is recounted for us in the Gospel of John. The twentieth chapter is most likely read in churches, from mainline to Protestant, every Easter. The stone is rolled away. The tomb is empty. Mary is hysterical because she has yet to realize that Christ is risen, just as the prophets of old and Jesus himself said it would be. She arrives at the tomb before the crack of dawn and finds the stone removed. She turns and runs, alerting John and Peter that something is up. Both of these men run to the tomb, John outrunning Peter. Interesting isn't it, that John highlights the fact that he is a faster runner that Peter? What's the significance? From a scriptural perspective, I don't know if there is any significance. From an allegorical perspective, it highlights the pride that overtakes us in our pursuit for God. Paul, in 1 Corinthians, says that we must run the race in such a way as to receive the prize. Some of us run the race and wipe out, then go directly to the podium to announce to everyone the reason why we dropped out of the race. Others lap the slower runners and ensure that everyone else knows it. "Look at me; I've lapped those slow runners more than once. They obviously don't want the prize as much as I do." From a spiritual perspective, we pump ourselves up as though we have it all together, or as if we're better because we are pursuing harder and running faster than anyone else.

It's my belief that every miracle follows three principles. Something happens that points to, or foretells, the miracle: the revelation. It could very well be miraculous in itself, but it isn't the miracle; it's just the revelation. For instance, when Jesus rose from the dead, He could have easily left the tomb; there was no need for the stone to be moved. The stone being moved wasn't the miracle, as miraculous as it was; it was the revelation of the miracle. The second principle is that, after the revelation of the miracle, there is the fullness of the miracle. The stone was the revelation of the fullness of the miraculous resurrection of Jesus Christ.

So here's John, proud of his running ability, pressing in hard, wanting to encounter or experience all that was going on down at the tomb, but as he arrived, he slowed his pace and stopped at the entrance of that tomb. Why he stopped we don't know—scripture doesn't record it. Was he frightened? Was it out of courtesy for Peter? Did he want to enter together? We don't know for sure, but I do know this: He didn't step into the fullness of the miracle, he stopped short at the revelation of the miracle. Many of us do that, too. We've been praying for God to move in our lives, to do something—to heal, to release, to save—and the revelation comes. A pastor speaks into us and says, "I believe that God is going to heal you ..." It's the revelation. Or a friend speaks life into you, "God told me that you will be blessed with riches ..." It's the revelation. It's not the fullness of the miracle; it's the revelation of the miracle. But we get excited. Do you know what God has promised to do or what the word of the Lord is over your life? We, like John, get stopped at the revelation. Don't stop at the revelation; step into the fullness of your miracle. Don't be excited about the revelation; keep running until the fullness of it has come. Peter raced by John and entered the fullness of the miracle, and then John followed. Together they stood in the very place that the miracle was made manifest, where life returned to a corpse, where the fullness of a miracle had occurred, yet they did not realize it, and the scripture records they returned home. When I speak of miracles, I don't presume that healing is the only miracle. Salvation is a miracle, too, worked by the cleansing blood of Jesus Christ. So even though they saw the revelation of the miracle and experienced the fullness of the miracle, in that they stepped into the empty tomb and were witness to the fact that it was indeed empty, they had not yet realized it.

As you read this, your condition may be the same as these disciples. You may have had a revelation that God was going to do something in you, through you or for you. You may have even stepped into the fullness of that miracle, but you have not come to the realization of that miracle yet.

After Peter and John left, Mary stood again at the entrance to the tomb. I imagine that the scene was anything but tranquil. She's crying and has yet to come to the realization of the miracle that has taken place. Just as her world is spinning out of control, a man whom she perceives to be the gardener comes, and she asks if he knows where the body of the Lord is. She's desperate; she's frustrated; she's tired; she's emotional; she's broken. She experiences every emotion that you can imagine rolled up into one, and all she needs is the realization of the miracle. And you sit on your leather sofa or on the hard park bench and, as you read this, every emotion possible has culminated into a ball of chaos, frustration, anger, hurt, loneliness, fatigue, pain or desire. All comes together and drives you to the same place that Mary was as she stood unknowingly, face to face, with her own realization. She stood face to face with that for which she sought passionately. Let me rephrase that. You stand face to face with that which you are passionately seeking.

A warm wind passes across your face, definitely not a strong wind. In fact, it's not even like wind at all; it's like someone is blowing on your face. Your eyes open, and you're intrigued by the dark, yet love-filled, eyes that are gazing back at you. You have a sudden recognition that you're consumed by this person, not inhibited and not confined, just surrounded. As your weary mind struggles for consciousness and awareness, you realize that this breath on your face isn't that of blowing. It's the exhale that comes after a word is gently spoken. You tune your ears to the sound, no longer distracted by the breath, or wind. Faintly you hear it. The chaos and hysteria that you had been experiencing, the anxiety and hurt, it's vanishing. The longing for the completion of your miracle, whatever it may be, becomes reality, and now you recognize the voice. Rabboni? He's calling your name. Gently and softly, wherever you are, whatever your situation, He's face to face, nose to nose, cheek to cheek with you, calling your name. It's the moment of your realization. That which you've been passionately and desperately searching for is right before you. The revelation, the fullness and the realization of your miracle has come, and you're renewed as you rediscover your childlike faith.

NOTES

[1] *John Hughes*: *National Lampoon's Christmas Vacation*, prod. and dir. Jeremiah Chechik, 97 min., Hughes Entertainment, 1989, DVD.

[2] Switchfoot, The Beautiful Letdown, "24" (Columbia Records, 2003)

[3] "About ALS." ALS Society of Canada. 1996-2006. als.ca. 23 Jan. 2006 <http://www.als.ca>.

[4] —Source: **Fathers' Involvement in Their Children's Schools.** National Center for Education Statistics. Washington DC: GPO, 1997.

[5] —Source: Hardy, Janet B. et al. **"Self Sufficiency at Ages 27 to 33 Years: Factors Present between Birth and 18 Years that Predict Educational Attainment Among children Born to Inner-city Families."** Pediatrics 99 (1997): 80-87.

9 781897 373002